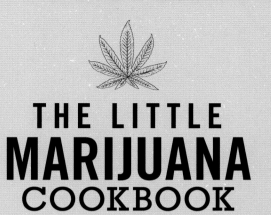

THE LITTLE
MARIJUANA
COOKBOOK

THE LITTLE
MARIJUANA
COOKBOOK

· · · · · · · · · · ·

OVER 40 EASY STONER RECIPES
FOR THE ULTIMATE HIGH

DANE NOON

First published in 2017 by Spruce,
an imprint of Octopus Publishing
Group Ltd
Carmelite House, 50 Victoria
Embankment
London EC4Y 0DZ
www.octopusbooks.co.uk
www.octopusbooksusa.com

An Hachette UK Company
www.hachette.co.uk

Distributed in the US by Hachette Book
Group, 1290 Avenue of the Americas
4th and 5th Floors, New York, NY 10104

Distributed in Canada by,
Canadian Manda Group
664 Annette St., Toronto, Ontario,
Canada M6S 2C8

ISBN 978-1-84601-545-8

A CIP catalogue record for this book
is available from the British Library.

Printed and bound in China

10 9 8 7 6

Standard level spoon measurements
are used in all recipes
1 tablespoon = 15 ml spoon
1 teaspoon = 5 ml spoon

All microwave information is
based on a 650 watt oven. Follow
manufacturer's instructions for an
oven with a different wattage.

Eggs should be medium unless
otherwise stated. This book contains
dishes made with lightly cooked eggs.
It is prudent for more vulnerable people
such as pregnant and nursing mothers,
invalids, the elderly, babies, and young
children to avoid uncooked or lightly
cooked dishes made with eggs.

This book includes dishes made
with nuts and nut derivatives. It is
advisable for people with known
allergic reactions to nuts and nut
derivatives or those who may be
potentially vulnerable to these
allergies, such as pregnant and
nursing mothers, invalids, the elderly,
babies, and children, to avoid dishes
made with these. It is prudent to
check the labels of all pre-prepared
ingredients for the possible inclusion
of nut derivatives.

CONTENTS

INTRODUCTION

If you've picked up this book, you're already a
convert to cannabis (or know someone who is),
so we don't need to extol the many virtues of the
magnificent weed. We could wax lyrical about its
claimed health benefits, its stress and relaxation
properties, and the wonders of getting high from
a plant...but we won't! Instead we'll concentrate on
the incredible versatility of the herb and introduce
you to a whole new way of enjoying your cheeba.

CANNABIS IN THE KITCHEN

If you've only ever rolled
and smoked your weed in a
carefully constructed blunt,
you're in for a culinary treat, as
we share a selection of
everyday recipes that will get
you high, with a hit that will

slowly develop and linger longer
than a few tokes on a spliff.

If you're not confident in the
kitchen and only use it in cases
of emergency hunger, don't
worry; the recipes in the book
are all quick and easy to
prepare, even for a novice

cook. You won't need any fancy ingredients or utensils to bake a batch of Caner Cookies (see page 56), or to rustle up a post-party Pizza (see page 36) for your mates. With just a few basic skills and a fairly well-stocked storecupboard and refrigerator, you can make all of the cannabis-infused sweet and savory recipes. Then sit back and enjoy the double delights of getting caned and gorging on munchies.

HERBAL HIGH

All the recipes use cannabutter or cannaoil as the essential ingredient (you can find instructions on how to make these on pages 8–13). You can use your choice of cannabis to prepare the butter or oil, but it's worth bearing in mind that the strain you use will dramatically affect the type and length of high you'll get when you eat the food. So, if you're looking for a pick-me-up that will literally blow your socks off, choose a sativa strain. On the other hand, if you don't plan on moving more than a few feet from your

couch for the foreseeable future, use an indica blend.

DAILY DOSE

Each cookie, cake, and bar recipe has the dose stated—others will be one dose per serving—so you know exactly how much you're making and eating. Obviously, if you cane a whole pizza, rather than sharing it, be aware that you've quite seriously upped the dosage and need to be prepared for an almighty high.

It's also worth remembering that ingesting cannabis is a very different way of getting high than smoking. When you toke on a spliff, you can wait a few minutes, see how you react and then go back for more. When you eat a plate of cannabutter cookies, you've taken your whole hit in, well, in one hit: there's no going back. The buzz will take longer to work its magic, but when it does you'll know about it. If you haven't experimented with culinary cannabis before, take it easy to start with and get to know your limits.

COOKING WITH
MARIJUANA

Cannabutter and cannaoil take a little while to prepare but, once you've made a batch, it should keep even the keenest caner in a ready supply for a number of weeks or months. You can keep small batches of each in the freezer, ready to take out when you've got a craving for a cannabis-laced dinner or snack.

CANNABUTTER

PREPARATION TIME: 30 minutes
COOKING TIME: about 6 hours

Makes 1lb cannabutter

1 oz decarbed weed (see page 15)
2 cups water
1 lb (4 sticks) unsalted butter

GRIND the weed to a fine powder using a strong grinder.

POUR the water into a heavy saucepan and bring to a boil over a medium-high heat. Once boiling, add in the butter and melt in the water. Reduce the heat to very low and whisk in the cannabis powder until thoroughly combined (there should be no lumps and nothing stuck to the bottom of the pan).

THE BUTTER and water will never mix completely, so it is the heat of the water that regulates the heat of the butter. Always make sure there is at least 1½–2 inches of water in the pan and the butter is floating on top.

COVER and cook at a very gentle simmer for 5–6 hours. Check every hour to ensure the simmer is not too strong and the butter has not reduced too much. If the mixture is reducing quickly, add a few extra tablespoons of water.

SIMMER the butter mixture until the fine bubbles stop appearing on top of the mix (these are an indication of the THC being released from the weed). Turn off the heat and allow to stand for 2–4 minutes.

MEANWHILE, line a large bowl with a square of cheesecloth, making sure the cheesecloth generously overhangs the edge of the bowl.

CAREFULLY pour the butter mixture into the bowl and strain off the bits of cannabis. Once you've strained the mixture and the cannabis material is collected in the cheesecloth, carefully squeeze it to extract as much of the butter solution as you can. This is what you want; you can discard the soggy cannabis by-product.

PUT the bowl of butter solution in your refrigerator and leave to cool for a few hours (or overnight) until the fats have completely separated from the water.

USE heavy-duty plastic wrap to remove the top slab of cannabutter from the bowl and then pat it dry with paper towel to remove any excess water. Divide the cannabutter into smaller, even-sized portions and wrap individually in plastic wrap. Store in an airtight container in the freezer. If frozen, the cannabutter won't lose potency but it is best used within 2–3 months.

CANNAOIL

PREPARATION TIME: 1 hour
COOKING TIME: 3–24 hours

Makes 3 cups of cannaoil

2 cups water
3 cups oil (use high-fat oils such as olive oil
   or coconut oil)
1 oz decarbed ground weed (see page 15)

BRING the water to a boil in a heavy saucepan over a medium-high heat. Once boiling, add in the oil, reduce the heat to very low and slowly add the ground weed. Simmer over a very low heat for at least 3 hours and a maximum of 24 hours. You'll know it is ready when the top of the mixture is thick and glossy.

MEANWHILE, line a large bowl with a square of cheesecloth, making sure the cheesecloth generously overhangs the edge of the bowl. Carefully pour the oil mixture into the bowl and strain off the bits of cannabis. Once you've strained the mixture and all the cannabis material is collected in the cheesecloth, carefully squeeze the cheesecloth to extract as much of the oil as you can.

PUT the bowl of butter solution in your refrigerator and leave to cool for a few hours (or overnight) until the oil has completely separated from the water.

ONCE cooled, carefully spoon off the oil and store in a sealed container in the refrigerator. Use within 6–8 weeks.

CANNABIS
COOKING TIPS
AND HERBAL HINTS

CHOOSE YOUR FLAVOR

Each strain of cannabis has its own distinct flavor and aroma and, although much of this will be lost when you add the other ingredients in a recipe, you'll still be able to pick out some of the subtle tasting notes. So make sure you choose the weed based on whether you're more likely be making sweet or savory recipes. Better still, make a batch of each then you're prepared for every eventuality.

It's also a good idea to start your culinary experiments with a lighter strain of weed, especially if you're likely to share the results of your baking with your mates. Not everyone can handle a momentous high—you can always eat another truffle or go back for a second of chili if you need a bigger hit. If you're planning a full menu of cannabis-infused recipes, take a break between courses so you can gauge the effects before carrying on.

HOW TO DECARB WEED

Cannabutter and cannaoil recipes use decarbed weed. This involves heating up the weed to create THC (tetrahydrocannabinol)—the chemical that gets you high. It's important not to miss out this crucial step or you'll be sitting around a plate of biscuit crumbs wondering why you're not floating up to the ceiling.

- Preheat the oven to 310°F.
- Grind the weed to a rough consistency and sprinkle it evenly into a heatproof pie dish.
- Cover and seal well with aluminum foil.
- Bake in the oven for about 10–15 minutes. When your kitchen smells like you've been skinning up all day, the weed is baked.
- Remove from the oven. Let it stand and cool with the foil on, until completely cooled.

STORING AND USING

Once you've made batches of cannabutter and cannaoil, it's important to label the individual portions with the strain of cannabis you used and the date you made the batch. You should also let your housemates know that you've stocked up the freezer with herbal high—not everyone will be thrilled to get loaded on a midweek dinner, thinking the innocent-looking block of butter in the freezer was just that.

Don't be tempted to add more active ingredient than the recipes call for; the amounts have been carefully calculated for the optimum high and to work with the other ingredients in the recipe. Double the dose on a whim and you'll end up with a wasted meal or a totally wasted bunch of friends.

HOW TO COME DOWN FROM A HIGH

Obviously, the ultimate aim of chomping into a Blunt Blondie (see page 72) or mopping up a bowl of Buzzing Bean and Rosemary Hummus (see page 32) with some tortilla chips is to get high. But what happens when you or your mates get carried away and take the high to a higher level? When you're feeling hungry and the food tastes good, it's easy to carry on eating and forget about the mind-altering main ingredient.

When you take cannabis in food, there's a time lapse between the weed hitting your system and you getting high. But there are a few things you can do to try and limit the effects and bring yourself back out of the stratosphere in a fairly gentle way.

- **Stay hydrated**—drink plenty of water but don't gulp it down and make yourself sick. Instead sip slowly from a glass of cold water.

- **Get some shut-eye**—sleep cures a lot of ills and if your high isn't too intense, you should be able to get over the worst of it by crashing out.

- **Quietly does it**—loud noise and bright lights can bring on paranoia so try and find a quiet space to relax and keep calm. Soft music, low lights, and some blankets and cushions will help to regulate your breathing and stop your high from escalating.

- **Take a walk**—if you're still able to stand and work your limbs, a gentle walk in the fresh air can help to bring you down from an unwanted high. Don't go out alone though; take a straight-headed mate with you in case you have a funny turn or wander too far from home and get lost.

- **Low-key conversation**—if you can't sleep and don't want to be alone, talking quietly with a trusted friend can really help to keep you calm and relaxed while you come down from your high.

SAFETY FIRST

It goes without saying that sharp kitchen implements and hot pans don't mix well with an intense buzz. When you're on the bud, your safety awareness, reaction times, and pain threshold will all be adversely affected so it's best to prepare all the weed feed you want before you start eating. A lot of the recipes in the book can be prepared ahead of time so you can cook with a clear head and stay well clear of the kitchen once you're buzzing later on.

SAVORY

HAM AND TOMATO
BUZZ BISCUITS

PREPARATION TIME: 20 minutes
COOKING TIME: 12–15 minutes

Makes 12
(2 per dose)

½ cup whole milk,
    plus extra to glaze
2 tablespoons sun-dried
    tomato paste
2 oz ham, finely diced
2 cups all-purpose flour
1 tablespoon baking powder
4 tablespoons cannabutter,
    chilled and diced
    (see page 9)
Ground paprika, to sprinkle

PREHEAT the oven to 425°F. Grease a baking sheet and line with nonstick parchment paper.

....

BEAT together the milk, tomato paste, and ham in a bowl. Put the flour and baking powder in a bowl or food processor. Add the butter and rub in with your fingertips, or process, until the mixture resembles fine breadcrumbs. Add the milk mixture and mix or blend briefly to a soft dough.

....

SHAPE the dough into a ball on a lightly floured surface, then roll out to ¾-inch thick. Cut out about 12 circles, using a 1½-inch plain cookie cutter, rerolling the trimmings to make more. Arrange slightly apart on the baking sheet, then lightly glaze with milk and sprinkle with paprika.

....

BAKE in the oven for 12–15 minutes, or until risen and golden. Transfer to a cooling rack. Serve warm or cold.

ZONE-OUT ZUCCHINI AND FETA BISCUITS

PREPARATION TIME: 20 minutes
COOKING TIME: 18–20 minutes

2 cups all-purpose flour
4½ teaspoons baking powder
1 teaspoon salt
¼ lb (1 stick) cannabutter, softened
  (see page 9)
½ teaspoon finely grated lemon zest
½ teaspoon dried thyme
½ teaspoon freshly ground black pepper
1⅓ cups coarsely grated zucchini
⅔ cup crumbled feta cheese
1 extra-large egg
1 tablespoon tomato paste
4–5 tablespoons milk

*Makes 12–14
(2 per dose)*

PREHEAT the oven to 400°F. Grease 2 baking sheets and line with nonstick parchment paper.

SIFT the flour, baking powder, and salt into a bowl. Add the cannabutter and rub in with your fingertips until the mixture resembles fine breadcrumbs. Stir in the lemon zest, thyme, black pepper, zucchini, and feta cheese.

BEAT together the egg and tomato paste in a bowl, then pour into the dry ingredients, adding just enough milk to form a soft, sticky batter.

DROP 12–14 mounds of the batter onto the baking sheets. Bake in the oven for 18–20 minutes until golden. Serve warm.

CANER
CHEDDAR BISCUITS

PREPARATION TIME: 20 minutes
COOKING TIME: 10 minutes

1 cup all-purpose flour,
  plus extra for dusting
1½ teaspoons baking powder
½ teaspoon dry mustard
Pinch of salt
1 teaspoon freshly ground
  black pepper

4 tablespoons cannabutter,
  softened (see page 9)
¼ cup grated sharp
  Cheddar cheese
1 extra-large egg yolk
1 tablespoon water

*Makes
about 20
(5 per dose)*

PREHEAT the oven to 400°F. Grease 2 baking sheets and line with nonstick parchment paper.

MIX together the flour, baking powder, mustard, salt, and black pepper in a bowl. Add the cannabutter and rub in with your fingertips until the mixture resembles fine breadcrumbs. Stir in the Cheddar, then add the egg yolk and water and mix to form a firm dough.

TURN the dough out onto a floured surface and knead lightly. Roll out to 1/8-inch thick, then stamp out about 20 circles or shapes, using a 2-inch cutter.

ARRANGE the circles on the baking sheets and bake in the oven for 10 minutes, or until lightly golden. Transfer to cooling racks.

SAVORY STONER
MUFFINS

PREPARATION TIME: 10 minutes
COOKING TIME: 20–25 minutes

1¼ cups self-rising flour
½ teaspoon salt
⅔ cup fine cornmeal
⅔ cup grated sharp Cheddar cheese
8 sun-dried tomatoes in oil,
    drained and chopped
2 tablespoons chopped basil
1 egg, lightly beaten
1¼ cups whole milk
4 tablespoons cannaoil (see page 12)
Butter, to serve

*Makes 8
(2 per dose)*

PREHEAT the oven to 325°F. Grease 8 muffin-pan holes.

SIFT the flour and salt into a bowl and stir in the corn flour, ½ cup of the Cheddar, the tomatoes, and basil. Make a well in the center.

BEAT the egg, milk, and cannaoil together in a separate bowl or pitcher, pour into the well and stir together until just combined. The batter should remain a little lumpy.

DIVIDE the batter between the muffin holes and sprinkle with the remaining Cheddar. Bake in the oven for 20–25 minutes until risen and golden. Allow to cool in the pan for 5 minutes, then transfer to a cooling rack to cool. Serve warm with butter.

MINI CHEESE AND CHIVE
CANNABIS CAKES

PREPARATION TIME: 10 minutes
COOKING TIME: 10–12 minutes

1⅔ cups self-rising flour
1 teaspoon baking powder
Good pinch of salt
½ cup grated sharp
   Cheddar cheese

4 tablespoons snipped chives
6 tablespoons cannabutter,
   melted (see page 9)
Scant ½ cup whole milk
1 egg, beaten

*Makes 20
(5 per dose)*

PREHEAT the oven to 400°F. Line 20 sections of 2 x 12-section mini muffin pans with mini paper baking cups.

PUT the flour, baking powder, and salt in a bowl. Stir in the Cheddar and chives until evenly mixed.

WHISK together the melted cannabutter, milk, and egg with a fork in a pitcher and add to the bowl. Stir well to form a thick paste. Divide the mixture between the paper baking cups.

BAKE in the oven for 10–12 minutes, or until risen and pale golden. Transfer to a cooling rack. Serve warm or cold.

SODA STONER
BREAD

PREPARATION TIME: 15 minutes
COOKING TIME: 30–35 minutes

3 cups all-purpose flour,
   plus extra for dusting
1 tablespoon granulated sugar
1 teaspoon baking soda
1 teaspoon baking powder
1 teaspoon salt
1 egg, beaten
1¼ cups buttermilk
3 teaspoons of canna olive oil
   (see page 12)

*Makes
1 loaf
(8 slices,
2 per dose)*

PREHEAT the oven to its highest setting. Dust a baking sheet with flour.

SIFT all the dry ingredients into a bowl. Whisk together the egg, buttermilk and cannaoil in a separate bowl then stir into the dry ingredients. Use your fingertips to form a dough.

TURN out the dough onto a floured surface and shape into a disc. Transfer to the baking sheet and make a large cross across the top of the dough, using a sharp knife. Dust with a little extra flour.

BAKE in the oven for 5 minutes, then reduce the temperature to 350°F and bake for an additional 25–30 minutes, or until it sounds hollow when tapped on the bottom.

BUZZING BEAN
AND ROSEMARY HUMMUS

PREPARATION TIME: 15 minutes, plus cooling
COOKING TIME: 10 minutes

6 tablespoons cannaoil, plus extra
to serve (see page 12)
4 shallots, finely chopped
2 large garlic cloves, crushed
1 teaspoon chopped rosemary, plus
extra sprigs to garnish

Grated zest and juice of ½ lemon
2 (13-oz) cans lima beans, drained
Salt and freshly ground black
pepper
Toasted ciabatta, to serve

HEAT the cannaoil in a skillet. Add the shallots, garlic, chopped rosemary, and lemon zest and cook over a low heat, stirring occasionally, for 10 minutes until the shallots are softened. Allow to cool.

TRANSFER the shallot mixture to a food processor, add the remaining ingredients and process until smooth.

SPREAD the hummus onto toasted ciabatta, garnish with rosemary sprigs and serve drizzled with cannaoil.

Serves
4–6

BLITZED
BAKED BEANS

PREPARATION TIME: 10 minutes
COOKING TIME: about 2 hours

Serves 4–6

2 teaspoons cannaoil (see page 12)
2 teaspoons cannabutter (see page 9)
2 (13-oz) cans borlotti beans, drained
1 garlic clove, crushed
1 onion, finely chopped
2 cups vegetable stock
1¼ cups passata (sieved tomatoes)
2 tablespoons molasses
Salt and freshly ground black pepper
2 tablespoons tomato paste
2 tablespoons dark brown sugar
1 tablespoon Dijon mustard
1 tablespoon red wine vinegar

PREHEAT the oven to 325°F.

PUT all the ingredients in a flameproof casserole and season with salt and pepper. Cover and bring slowly to a boil on the hob.

TRANSFER to the oven and bake for 1½ hours. Uncover and bake for an extra 30 minutes until the sauce is syrupy.

VEG-OUT VEGGIE
FRITTATTA

PREPARATION TIME: 10 minutes
COOKING TIME: 15 minutes

6 eggs
5 tablespoons grated Parmesan
   cheese
1 bunch of watercress, tough stalks
   removed

3 teaspoons cannabutter
   (see page 9)
3 cups mushrooms, thinly sliced
Salt and freshly ground
   black pepper

BEAT the eggs in a bowl with a fork. Stir in the Parmesan, watercress, and plenty of salt and pepper.

MELT the cannabutter in a heavy skillet. Add the mushrooms and fry quickly for 3 minutes. Pour in the egg mixture and gently stir the ingredients together.

REDUCE the heat to its lowest setting and fry gently until the mixture is lightly set and the underside is golden when the edge of the frittata is lifted with a palette knife. Transfer to a large plate and serve in slices.

Serves
3–4

HERB-LOVER'S PIZZA

PREPARATION TIME: 25 minutes
COOKING TIME: 15–18 minutes

FOR THE DOUGH:
2 cups self-rising flour,
    plus extra for dusting
3 tablespoons cannaoil
    (see page 12)
2 tablespoons cannabutter,
    melted (see page 9)
1 teaspoon salt
Scant ½ cup water

FOR THE TOPPING:
Scant ½ cup cream cheese
Scant ½ cup crème fraîche
2 tablespoons chopped rosemary
3 tablespoons olive oil
1 large onion, thinly sliced
12 oz baby spinach
Salt and freshly ground
    black pepper

Serves
4

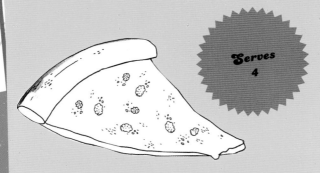

PREHEAT the oven to 450°F. Grease a large baking sheet.

PUT the flour in a bowl with the cannaoil, cannabutter, and salt. Add the water and mix to a soft dough, adding a little more water if the dough is too dry.

ON a lightly floured surface, roll out the dough into a round, about 11 inches in diameter. Transfer to the baking sheet and bake in the oven for 3–4 minutes, until a crust has formed.

MAKE the topping. Beat the cream cheese, crème fraîche, and chopped rosemary together in a bowl and season with salt and pepper. Heat the oil in a skillet and fry the onion for 3–4 minutes until softened. Stir in the spinach and a little salt and pepper, and cook for about 1 minute until the spinach has just wilted.

PILE the spinach onto the pizza base, spreading it out to about ½ inch from the edge. Put spoonfuls of the cheese mixture on top of the spinach, then bake the pizza for 8 minutes or until turning golden.

MARIJUANA
MOUSSAKA

PREPARATION TIME: 15 minutes
COOKING TIME: 45–50 minutes, plus standing

⅔ cup brown or green
   lentils, rinsed
1 (14-oz) can chopped tomatoes
2 garlic cloves, crushed
½ teaspoon dried oregano
Pinch of ground (or freshly grated)
   nutmeg
⅔ cup vegetable stock
3–4 tablespoons cannaoil
   (see page 12)
1 small eggplant, sliced
1 onion, finely chopped
Mixed leaf salad, to serve

FOR THE CHEESE TOPPING:
1 egg
⅔ cup full-fat cream cheese
Pinch of ground (or freshly grated)
   nutmeg
Salt and freshly ground
   black pepper

Serves
4

PREHEAT the oven to 400°F.

PUT the lentils in a saucepan with the tomatoes, garlic, oregano, and nutmeg.

POUR in the stock. Bring to a boil, then reduce the heat and simmer for 20 minutes until the lentils are tender but not mushy.

MEANWHILE, heat the cannaoil in a skillet and lightly sauté the eggplant slices and onion until the onion is soft and the eggplant is golden on both sides.

LAYER the eggplant mixture and lentil mixture alternately in an ovenproof dish.

MAKE the topping. In a bowl, beat together the egg, cream cheese, and nutmeg until combined. Season with salt and pepper. Pour the topping over the moussaka and cook in the oven for 20–25 minutes until golden and bubbling. Remove from the oven and let stand for 5 minutes before serving with a mixed leaf salad.

GET STEWED
CHORIZO AND BEAN STEW

PREPARATION TIME: 10 minutes
COOKING TIME: 25–30 minutes

4 tablespoons cannaoil
  (see page 12)
8 oz chorizo sausage, diced
1 onion, thickly sliced
1 red bell pepper, cored, deseeded,
  and thickly sliced
2 garlic cloves, chopped or sliced
  (optional)
2 (14-oz) cans chopped tomatoes

1 teaspoon dried oregano or
  mixed herbs (optional)
2 (15-oz) cans beans (such as
  cannellini or lima beans),
  drained
Salt and freshly ground black
  pepper
2 tablespoons chopped parsley,
  to garnish (optional)

HEAT the cannaoil in a large saucepan or skillet and cook the chorizo, onion, bell pepper, and garlic for about 10 minutes until the vegetables are softened.

ADD the tomatoes, herbs, and beans. Cover and simmer gently for 15–18 minutes until the stew is rich and thick.

SEASON with salt and pepper, ladle into bowls, and serve garnished with chopped parsley, if liked.

Serves
4

CHILI CON CANNABIS

PREPARATION TIME: 15 minutes
COOKING TIME: 50 minutes

1 tablespoon vegetable oil
1 red onion, finely chopped
1 garlic clove, finely chopped
8 oz extra-lean ground beef
2 tablespoons cannabutter (see page 9)
1 red bell pepper, cored, deseeded, and
    diced
1 (14-oz) can chopped tomatoes
1 tablespoon tomato paste
2 teaspoons chili powder
1 cup beef stock
1 (15-oz) can red kidney beans, drained
Salt and freshly ground black pepper
Cooked brown rice, to serve

HEAT the oil in a heavy, nonstick saucepan over a medium heat. Add the onion and garlic and cook for 5 minutes until beginning to soften. Add the beef and cook for 5 minutes, or until browned all over.

STIR in the cannabutter, bell pepper, chopped tomatoes, tomato paste, chili powder, and stock. Bring to a boil, then reduce the heat and simmer gently for 30 minutes.

ADD the kidney beans and cook for a further 5 minutes. Season with salt and pepper and serve with brown rice.

Serves
2

MUNCHIE
MEATBALLS

PREPARATION TIME: 20 minutes, plus soaking
COOKING TIME: 1 hour

1 slice white bread, crusts removed
½ onion, grated
1½ lb ground minced pork
½ lb ground veal or chicken
3 garlic cloves, crushed
Handful of parsley, chopped
1 egg
2 tablespoons olive oil
Salt and freshly ground
    black pepper

FOR THE TOMATO SAUCE:
2 tablespoons cannaoil
    (see page 12)
1 onion, finely chopped
2 garlic cloves, crushed
1 teaspoon sweet smoked paprika
½ cup dry white wine
1 (14-oz) can chopped tomatoes
1 thyme sprig

*Serves
4–6*

BREAK up the bread and put in a bowl. Add enough water to cover, then leave to soak for 5 minutes. Drain, then squeeze to remove the excess water and return to the bowl.

SQUEEZE the grated onion to remove most of the juice and add to the bread. Stir in the meat, garlic, and parsley. Add the egg, season with salt and pepper and mix together. Shape the mixture into walnut-sized balls using wet hands.

HEAT the oil in a large skillet, add the meatballs in 2 batches and fry for 5 minutes, turning occasionally, until golden all over. Set aside.

MAKE the sauce. Heat the cannaoil in a large saucepan, add the onion and cook for 5 minutes until softened. Stir in the garlic and paprika and cook for a further 30 seconds. Pour in the wine and cook for 2 minutes until reduced by half.

ADD the tomatoes and thyme, season with salt and pepper, and cook over a low heat for 10 minutes. Add the meatballs to the sauce and simmer for 30 minutes until the meatballs are cooked through, adding a little water if necessary.

POTHEAD
PARMIGIANA

PREPARATION TIME: 30 minutes
COOKING TIME: 1 hour 10 minutes, plus standing

6 eggplants
4 tablespoons cannaoil
   (see page 12)
2 cups grated Cheddar cheese
½ cup grated Parmesan cheese
Salt

FOR THE TOMATO SAUCE:
2 tablespoons cannaoil (see page 12)
1 large onion, chopped
2 garlic cloves, finely chopped
1 (14-oz) can chopped tomatoes
Salt and freshly ground black pepper
Green salad, to serve
Crusty bread, to serve

Serves
6

PREHEAT the oven to 400°F.

MAKE the tomato sauce. Heat the cannaoil in a skillet and fry the onion for 5 minutes. Add the garlic and tomatoes and cook gently for 10 minutes. Season with salt and pepper and keep warm.

TRIM the ends from the eggplants and cut them lengthwise into thick slices. Sprinkle generously with salt and set aside for 10 minutes. Rinse, drain, and pat dry on paper towels.

BRUSH the eggplant slices with cannaoil and arrange them on 2 large baking sheets. Roast the in the oven for 10 minutes on each side until golden and tender. Do not turn off the oven.

SPOON a little of the tomato sauce into an ovenproof dish and top with a layer of roasted eggplant and some of the Cheddar. Continue with the layers, finishing with Cheddar. Sprinkle over the Parmesan and bake in the oven for 30 minutes until bubbling and golden.

REMOVE from the oven and allow to stand for 5–10 minutes. Serve with a crisp green salad and crusty bread to mop up the juices.

SWEET

TOKER'S
TRAYBAKE

PREPARATION TIME: 10 minutes
COOKING TIME: 25 minutes

¼ lb (1 stick) cannabutter
  (see page 9)
4 tablespoons unsalted butter
¼ cup superfine or
  granulated sugar

⅔ cup light corn syrup
Finely grated zest of 2 lemons
2¾ cups rolled oats
½ cup golden raisins

*Makes 12
(2 per dose)*

PREHEAT the oven to 350°F. Grease an 8 x 8 x 2-inch baking pan and line with nonstick parchment paper.

PUT the butters, sugar, corn syrup, and lemon zest in a saucepan and heat gently until the butter has melted. Remove from the heat and stir in the oats and raisins. Mix well.

SPOON the mixture into the baking pan and level the surface with the back of a spoon.

BAKE in the oven for about 20 minutes until turning golden. Let cool in the pan for 10 minutes then transfer to a cooling rack to cool completely. Peel off the lining paper and cut into squares.

BANANA BLUNT
MUFFINS

**Makes 12
(2 per dose)**

PREPARATION TIME: 15 minutes
COOKING TIME: 18–22 minutes

1 cup banana chips, crushed
1⅔ cups all-purpose flour
2 teaspoons baking powder
½ teaspoon ground cinnamon
    (optional)
¼ cup firmly packed dark brown
    or granulated sugar

⅔ cup wheat bran
2 eggs
4 tablespoons cannabutter,
    melted (see page 9)
½ cup buttermilk
1 ripe banana, mashed

PREHEAT the oven to 350°F. Grease or line a 12-cup muffin pan with paper muffin cups.

PUT the banana chips in a bowl with the remaining dry ingredients. Whisk together the wet ingredients separately.

POUR the wet ingredients into the dry ingredients and stir until just combined.

DIVIDE the batter between the muffin cups and bake in the oven for 18–22 minutes until risen and firm to the touch. Transfer to cooling racks and serve warm.

RAISIN ZONE-OUT
TRAY CAKE

PREPARATION TIME: 10 minutes
COOKING TIME: 20–25 minutes

⅓ cup light corn syrup
¼ lb (1 stick) cannabutter, softened
   (see page 9)
1 cup all-purpose flour
1 teaspoon baking powder
⅔ cup granulated sugar

2 extra-large eggs
1 teaspoon vanilla extract
   (optional)
½ cup raisins
Light cream, whipped cream, or
   ice cream, to serve (optional)

PREHEAT the oven to 400°F. Grease a 10 x 8 x 2-inch baking pan.

POUR the corn syrup into the baking pan. Beat the remaining ingredients together in a bowl until pale and creamy. Spoon over the syrup coating. Bake in the oven for 20–25 minutes, or until risen and golden.

SERVE with light cream, whipped cream, or ice cream, if liked.

Makes 6
(1 per dose)

CANNABUTTER
SHORTBREAD

PREPARATION TIME: 10 minutes
COOKING TIME: 10–12 minutes

¼ lb (1 stick) cannabutter, softened,
    plus extra for greasing (see page 9)
¼ cup superfine or granulated sugar
⅔ cup all-purpose flour
¾ cup cornstarch
Turbinado sugar, for sprinkling

*Serves 12
(2 per dose)*

PREHEAT the oven to 400°F. Grease a 12 x 8 x 2-inch baking pan.

BEAT together the cannabutter and sugar in a bowl until pale and fluffy. Stir in the flour and cornstarch and combine to form a dough.

PRESS the dough into the baking pan and prick all over with a fork. Sprinkle with the turbinado sugar. Bake in the oven for 10–12 minutes until golden.

LET COOL in the baking pan for 2–3 minutes then mark into 12 bars. Leave in the pan for another 5 minutes, then transfer to a cooling rack to cool completely.

CHOCOLATE CHIP
CANER COOKIE

PREPARATION TIME: 10 minutes
COOKING TIME: 15–18 minutes

¼ lb (1 stick) cannabutter,
  softened (see page 9)
¾ cup firmly packed light
  brown sugar
1 teaspoon vanilla extract
1 egg, lightly beaten
1 tablespoon whole milk
1⅔ cups all-purpose flour
1 teaspoon baking powder
8 oz semisweet
  chocolate chips

*Makes 16
(2–3 per dose)*

PREHEAT the oven to 350°F. Grease a large baking sheet and line with nonstick baking parchment.

....

BEAT together the cannabutter and sugar in a bowl until pale and fluffy. Mix in the vanilla, then gradually beat in the egg.

....

STIR in the milk. Sift in the flour and baking powder, then fold in to combine. Stir in the chocolate chips.

....

ROLL teaspoons of the dough into walnut-sized balls, then arrange slightly apart on the baking sheet and flatten gently with a fork.

....

BAKE in the oven for 15–18 minutes until risen and golden. Transfer to a cooling rack.

PEANUT BUTTER
COMEDOWN COOKIES

PREPARATION TIME: 15 minutes
COOKING TIME: 15–18 minutes

⅓ cup chunky peanut butter
½ cup superfine or granulated sugar
6 tablespoons cannabutter, softened
  (see page 9)
1 egg, beaten
¾ teaspoon all-purpose flour
¾ teaspoon baking powder
¼ cup chopped salted peanuts

*Makes 18–20
(4–5 per dose)*

PREHEAT the oven to 350°F. Grease a large baking sheet and line with nonstick baking parchment.

BEAT together the peanut butter, sugar, and cannabutter in a bowl until well combined. Add the egg, flour, and baking powder and mix to a paste.

ROLL teaspoons of the dough into walnut-sized balls, then arrange slightly apart on the baking sheet and flatten gently with a fork. Sprinkle the chopped peanuts over the cookies.

BAKE in the oven for 15–18 minutes until risen and golden. Transfer to a cooling rack.

FUDGE AND OAT
CROSSFADE COOKIES

PREPARATION TIME: 20 minutes
COOKING TIME: 10–12 minutes

¼ lb (1 stick) cannabutter (see page 9)
1 tablespoon honey
1 cup rolled oats
1 teaspoon vanilla extract
1 teaspoon baking soda
1 cup all-purpose flour
½ cup firmly packed light brown sugar
2 oz miniature fudge chunks

*Makes
18–20
(3 per dose)*

PREHEAT the oven to 400°F. Grease 2 large baking sheets and line with nonstick baking parchment.

PUT the cannabutter, honey, oats, vanilla extract, and baking soda in a saucepan over a low heat and warm gently until the butter has melted. Stir well, then let cool for 5 minutes.

SCRAPE the dough into a large bowl and stir in the flour and sugar. Add the fudge chunks and mix until combined. Roll teaspoons of the dough into 18–20 balls then arrange slightly apart on the baking sheets. Flatten gently with a fork.

BAKE in the oven for 10–12 minutes until risen and golden. Let sit on the sheets for 1 minute then transfer to cooling racks to harden.

LIFT-OFF
GINGER CAKE

PREPARATION TIME: 20 minutes
COOKING TIME: 1¼ hours

4 cups self-rising flour
1 tablespoon ground ginger
½ teaspoon baking soda
½ teaspoon salt
Generous ¾ cup light brown sugar
¾ cup cannabutter (see page 9)
Scant ¾ cup molasses
Scant ¾ cup light corn syrup
1¼ cups whole milk
1 egg, lightly beaten

Serves 12

PREHEAT the oven to 325°F. Grease a 12 x 8 x 2-inch baking pan and line with nonstick parchment paper.

....

SIFT the flour, ground ginger, baking soda, and salt into a bowl. Put the sugar, cannabutter, molasses, and corn syrup into a saucepan and heat gently until the butter has melted and the sugar dissolved.

....

POUR the liquid into the dry ingredients. Add the milk and egg and beat with a wooden spoon until smooth. Pour the mixture into the baking pan.

....

BAKE in the oven for 1¼ hours, or until a skewer inserted into the center comes out clean. Let cool in the pan for 10 minutes then turn out onto a cooling rack. Wrap the cooled cake in aluminum foil to store.

OATMEAL
STONER SLICES

PREPARATION TIME: 15 minutes
COOKING TIME: 20 minutes

7 oz (1¾ sticks) cannabutter,
    plus extra for greasing
    (see page 9)
⅔ cup turbinado sugar
⅓ cup agave nectar or honey
½ cup sweetened
    condensed milk
3½ cups rolled oats
⅔ cup all-purpose flour
1 teaspoon baking powder
Pinch of salt
1 teaspoon allspice (optional)

*Makes 12–16
(1–2 per dose)*

PREHEAT the oven to 350°F. Grease a 12 x 8 x 2-inch baking pan and line with nonstick parchment paper.

PUT the cannabutter, sugar, agave nectar or honey, and condensed milk into a large saucepan. Heat gently, stirring occasionally, until the butter has melted and the sugar dissolved.

MIX together the remaining ingredients in a bowl, then pour into the warm syrup and stir until combined.

SPOON the mixture into the baking pan and level the surface with the back of a spoon.

BAKE in the oven for 15 minutes until turning golden.

LET cool in the pan for 5 minutes then mark into 12–16 squares or bars. Leave in the pan for another 5 minutes, then transfer to a cooling rack to cool completely. Peel off the lining paper and cut into squares.

ROCK CANNABIS CAKES

PREPARATION TIME: 15 minutes
COOKING TIME: 15–20 minutes

¼ lb (1 stick) cannabutter,
    softened (see page 9)
½ cup turbinado or muscovado sugar,
    plus extra for sprinkling
1¾ cups all-purpose flour
1¾ teaspoons baking powder
2 teaspoons ground allspice
1 egg
⅔ cup buttermilk
1¼ cups raisins

*Makes 18–20
(3 per dose)*

PREHEAT the oven to 375°F. Grease 2 large baking sheets
and line with nonstick baking parchment.

BEAT together the cannabutter and sugar in a bowl until
pale and fluffy. Add the remaining ingredients and mix until
well combined.

USING 2 forks, put small mounds of the dough, spaced
slightly apart, on the baking sheets. Sprinkle with sugar.

BAKE in the oven for 15–20 minutes until deep golden.
Transfer to a cooling rack. Serve on the same day.

MALTY RAISIN
SPACE CAKES

PREPARATION TIME: 10 minutes, plus standing
COOKING TIME: 20 minutes

¼ lb (1 stick) cannabutter,
  cut into pieces (see page 9)
2 cups bran flakes
1 cup whole milk
½ cup agave nectar or
  light maple syrup
Heaping ¾ cup raisins
1¼ cups self-rising flour
½ teaspoon baking powder

*Makes 12
(2 per dose)*

PREHEAT the oven to 350°F. Line a 12-section cupcake pan with paper baking cups.

PUT the cannabutter and bran flakes in a heatproof bowl. Bring the milk almost to the boil in a saucepan and pour into the bowl. Let stand for 10–15 minutes, until the bran flakes are very soft and the mixture has cooled slightly, then stir in the agave nectar or maple syrup and raisins.

SIFT the flour and baking powder into the bowl and stir until just mixed. Divide the cake mixture between the paper cups.

BAKE in the oven for 20 minutes, or until slightly risen and just firm to the touch. Transfer to a cooling rack.

VANILLA
CANNA-CUPCAKES

PREPARATION TIME: 10 minutes
COOKING TIME: 20 minutes

¼ lb (1 stick) cannabutter, softened
   (see page 9)
⅔ cup superfine sugar
1⅓ cups self-rising flour
3 eggs
1 teaspoon vanilla extract

*Makes 12
(1–2 per
dose)*

PREHEAT the oven to 350°F. Line a 12-section cupcake pan
with paper baking cups, or stand 12 silicone cups on
a baking sheet.

PUT all the ingredients in a bowl and beat with a handheld
electric mixer for 1–2 minutes until light and creamy. Divide
the cake mixture between the paper or silicone cups.

BAKE in the oven for 20 minutes, or until risen and just firm
to the touch. Transfer to a cooling rack.

BLUNT
BLONDIES

PREPARATION TIME: 20 minutes, plus cooling
COOKING TIME: 25–30 minutes

1 lb 1 oz white chocolate, roughly chopped
5 tablespoons cannabutter (see page 9)
3 eggs
Generous ¾ cup superfine sugar
1½ cups self-rising flour
1¼ cups macadaemia nuts, roughly chopped
1 teaspoon vanilla extract

*Makes 18
(3 per dose)*

PREHEAT the oven to 375°F. Grease a 12 x 8 x 2-inch baking pan and line the base with nonstick parchment paper.

SET aside 14 oz of the white chocolate. Melt the remaining chocolate and cannabutter in a small heatproof bowl set over a saucepan of simmering water. Cool slightly.

BEAT the eggs and sugar together in a bowl and gradually beat in the melted chocolate. Sift the flour over the mixture and fold in, together with the macadamia nuts, reserved chocolate, and vanilla extract.

POUR the mixture into the baking pan and bake in the oven for 25–30 minutes until the center is only just firm to the touch. Let cool in the pan for 10 minutes before cutting into 18 squares.

LIFT the blondies out carefully with a palette knife. Serve slightly warm or cool completely and store in an airtight container between layers of parchment paper.

CHOCOLATE
CANER BROWNIE

PREPARATION TIME: 20 minutes, plus cooling
COOKING TIME: 25–30 minutes

7 oz bittersweet chocolate,
    broken into chunks
7 oz (1¾ sticks) cannabutter
    (see page 9)
3 eggs
1 teaspoon vanilla extract
1 tablespoon strong espresso
    (or 1 tablespoon coffee granules
    dissolved in 1 tablespoon hot water)
1 cup superfine sugar
¾ cup all-purpose flour
¼ teaspoon salt
⅔ cup walnuts, roughly chopped
⅔ cup pecan nuts, roughly chopped
Heavy cream, to serve

*Make 12–16
(2 per dose)*

PREHEAT the oven to 350°F. Grease a 12 x 8 x 2-inch baking pan and line the base with nonstick parchment paper.

MELT the chocolate and cannabutter in a small heatproof bowl set over a saucepan of simmering water. Let cool for 5 minutes.

BEAT the eggs in a bowl with the vanilla extract, espresso, and sugar until well combined, then beat in the melted chocolate mix. Add the flour and salt and beat until smooth. Stir in the nuts. Pour the brownie mixture into the baking pan.

BAKE in the oven for 25–30 minutes. Be careful not to overcook: the sides should be firm but the center should still be slightly soft. Let cool in the pan for 10 minutes before cutting into squares.

LIFT the brownies out carefully with a palette knife. Serve slightly warm with heavy cream, or cool completely and store in an airtight container between layers of parchment paper.

MARY JANE
CHOCOLATE CAKE

PREPARATION TIME: 20 minutes
COOKING TIME: 45 minutes

10 oz dark chocolate,
    broken into pieces
6 oz (1½ sticks) cannabutter
    (see page 9)
2 teaspoons vanilla extract
5 eggs

6 tablespoons heavy cream,
    plus extra to serve (optional)
1 cup superfine sugar
Handful of blueberries
Handful of raspberries

**Serves 8
(1 slice
per dose)**

PREHEAT the oven to 350°F. Grease an 8 x 8 x 2-inch baking pan and line with nonstick parchment paper.

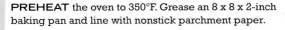

MELT the chocolate and cannabutter in a small heatproof bowl set over a saucepan of simmering water. Remove from the heat and add the vanilla extract.

BEAT the eggs, cream, and sugar together for 3–4 minutes (the mixture will remain fairly runny), then fold into the chocolate mixture.

POUR the batter into the baking pan and bake in the oven for 45 minutes, or until the top forms a crust. Allow the cake to cool and then run a knife around the edges to loosen it from the pan.

TURN out the cake onto a serving plate and top with the blueberries and raspberries. Serve with extra cream, if liked.

CANNA CHOC CHIP
MUG CAKE

*Serves 1
(1 cake
per dose)*

PREPARATION TIME: 3 minutes
COOKING TIME: 1¾ minutes

3 tablespoons cannabutter,
   softened (see page 9)
3 tablespoons superfine sugar
1 egg
¼ teaspoon vanilla extract

3 tablespoons self-rising flour
2 tablespoons bittersweet or milk
   chocolate chips
Sifted cocoa powder, for dusting

BEAT together the cannabutter and sugar in a 12 fl oz microwave-safe mug. Add the egg, vanilla extract, and flour and beat until smooth.

MICROWAVE on full power for about 45 seconds or until the mixture is beginning to set. Scatter half the chocolate chips over the cake and stir. Scatter over the remaining chocolate chips and stir again.

MICROWAVE on full power for 1 minute more, or until just firm to touch. Serve dusted with cocoa powder.

HOT COFFEE
REEFER MUG CAKE

PREPARATION TIME: 5 minutes
COOKING TIME: 1½ minutes

½ teaspoon instant coffee
   granules or powder
½ teaspoon boiling water
3 tablespoons cannabutter,
   softened (see page 9)
2½ tablespoons superfine sugar
⅛ teaspoon ground cinnamon

Generous pinch of chili powder,
   plus extra for dusting
1 egg
3 tablespoons self-rising flour
1 tablespoon chopped pecan nuts
Heavy cream, to serve (optional)

BEAT the coffee and water in a 12 fl oz microwave-safe mug and stir to mix. Add the cannabutter, sugar, cinnamon, chili powder, egg, flour, and nuts and beat together until well mixed.

MICROWAVE on full power for 1½ minutes, or until the surface feels just firm to the touch and a skewer inserted into the center comes out clean. Dust with chili powder and serve with heavy cream, if liked.

*Serves 1
(1 cake
per dose)*

GANJA BANANA
MUG CAKE

PREPARATION TIME: 3 minutes
COOKING TIME: 2 minutes

*Makes 1
(1 cake
per dose)*

1 small very ripe banana
1 egg
¼ teaspoon ground mixed spice
2 tablespoons cannabutter,
    softened (see page 9)
3 tablespoons self-rising flour
1 tablespoon chopped walnuts
    or pecan nuts
2 tablespoons light brown sugar
Maple syrup, to drizzle

MASH the banana in a 12 fl oz microwave-safe mug until almost completely puréed. Add the egg, mixed spice, cannabutter, flour, half the nuts, and the sugar and beat together until well mixed.

MICROWAVE on full power for 2 minutes, or until just firm to the touch and a skewer inserted into the center comes out clean. Serve scattered with the remaining nuts and drizzled with maple syrup.

HIGH CHAI
MUG CAKE

PREPARATION TIME: 3 minutes
COOKING TIME: 2 minutes

1 chai teabag
5 tablespoons boiling water
4 tablespoons mixed dried fruit
2 dried figs, sliced
¼ teaspoon ground mixed spice
4 teaspoons cannaoil (see page 12)
3 tablespoons self-rising whole-wheat flour
1 tablespoon turbinado sugar,
   plus extra to sprinkle

*Makes 1
(1 cake
per dose)*

PUT the teabag and water in a 7 fl oz microwave-safe mug
and stir for 15 seconds. Squeeze the teabag and discard.

ADD the dried fruits and mixed spice and microwave on full
power for 30 seconds. Add the canna oil, flour, and sugar and
stir until mixed.

MICROWAVE on full power for 1½ minutes, or until firm to
the touch and a skewer inserted into the center comes out
clean. Sprinkle with a little extra sugar and serve.

POT-LOVER'S
PANCAKE

PREPARATION TIME: 10 minutes, plus resting (optional)
COOKING TIME: 15–25 minutes

1 cup buckwheat flour
Pinch of salt
3 eggs, lightly beaten
3 teaspoons cannaoil
   (see page 12)
1¼ cups milk
Light olive oil, vegetable oil,
   or butter, for greasing

*Makes 8–10
(3 per dose)*

PUT the flour and salt in a bowl and make a well in the center. Add the eggs, cannaoil, and a little of the milk and whisk together, gradually incorporating the flour. Add the remaining milk and mix to a smooth paste. Pour into a pitcher and allow to rest, if liked.

....

PUT a little oil or butter into a 7-inch pancake pan or heavy skillet and heat until it starts to smoke. Pour off the excess and pour a little batter into the pan, tilting the pan until the base is coated in a thin layer. (If you prefer, use a small ladle to measure the batter into the pan.) Cool for 1–2 minutes until the underside is turning golden.

....

FLIP the pancake with a palette knife and cook for a further 30–45 seconds until golden on the second side. Slide the pancake out of the pan and make the remaining pancakes, greasing the pan as necessary.

BAKED
BANANAS

PREPARATION TIME: 10 minutes
COOKING TIME: 10 minutes

8 bananas, peeled
2 tablespoons lemon juice
8 tablespoons light brown sugar
¼ cup cannabutter, softened
    (see page 9)
1 teaspoon ground cinnamon

FOR THE RUM MASCARPONE CREAM:
8 oz mascarpone cheese
2 tablespoons rum
1–2 tablespoons granulated sugar

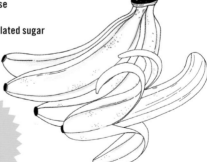

Serves 8

PUT each banana on a double piece of foil. Drizzle over the lemon juice and sprinkle 1 tablespoon of the brown sugar on each banana.

BEAT together the cannabutter and cinnamon in a bowl until creamy, then spoon over the bananas. Wrap each banana tightly in the foil and cook over a barbecue or under a preheated medium-hot broiler for 10 minutes.

MEANWHILE, make the rum mascarpone cream. Mix together the mascarpone, rum, and sugar in a bowl.

UNWRAP the bananas and slice thickly. Serve immediately with the rum mascarpone cream.

APPLE CRISP
MUNCHIES

PREPARATION TIME: 10 minutes
COOKING TIME: 10–15 minutes

6 cooking apples (about 2 lb),
    peeled, cored, and thickly sliced
2 tablespoons butter
2 tablespoons granulated sugar
1 tablespoon lemon juice
2 tablespoons water

FOR THE CRUMB TOPPING:

4 tablespoons cannabutter
    (see page 9)
1½ cups fresh whole-wheat
    breadcrumbs
3 tablespoons pumpkin seeds
2 tablespoons packed
    dark brown sugar

Serves 4

PUT the apples in a saucepan with the butter, sugar, lemon juice, and water. Cover and simmer for 8–10 minutes until softened. Remove from the heat.

....

FOR the crumb topping, melt the cannabutter in a skillet, add the breadcrumbs, and cook over a medium heat until light golden. Add the pumpkin seeds and cook for another 1 minute. Remove from the heat and stir in the brown sugar.

....

SPOON the apple mixture into bowls, sprinkle with the crumb topping, and serve.

CANER'S
HOT CHOCOLATE

PREPARATION TIME:
30 minutes

2¼ cups milk
1 tablespoon cannabutter
   (see page 9)
Scant ½ cup ground almonds
3½ tablespoons superfine sugar
2 teaspoons ground cinnamon
1 vanilla pod, split down
   the center
4 oz semisweet chocolate,
   broken into chunks

PUT the milk, cannabutter, ground almonds, sugar, cinnamon, and vanilla pod in a medium saucepan. Bring to a boil over a low heat. Take off the heat and let infuse for 20 minutes.

POUR the mixture through a very fine sieve into a clean saucepan, squeezing out the milk from the ground almonds.

ADD the chocolate to the milk and stir over a low heat until the chocolate has melted. Serve immediately.

SALTED CARAMEL
POTCORN

PREPARATION TIME: 5 minutes
COOKING TIME: 10 minutes

Serves 4

1 teaspoon sunflower oil
¼ cup popping corn
1 cup granulated sugar
5 tablespoons cannabutter (see page 9)
Sea salt flakes

HEAT the oil in a large lidded saucepan. Add the popping corn, cover, and heat, shaking the pan frequently until the corn has all popped. Transfer to a large sheet of nonstick parchment paper.

PUT the sugar into a saucepan and heat over a low heat until the sugar has dissolved. Simmer until golden, then stir in the cannabutter. Drizzle the caramel over the popcorn and sprinkle with sea salt.

TANKED-UP
TRUFFLES

PREPARATION TIME: 20 minutes, plus chilling

½ cup plus 2 tablespoons
heavy cream
8 oz bittersweet chocolate, finely
chopped
2 tablespoons cannabutter, diced
(see page 9)

2 tablespoons liqueur (brandy,
rum, Cointreau, or coffee
liqueur)
Unsweetened cocoa, for dusting

*Makes 6
(2 per dose)*

BRING the cream just to a boil in a small saucepan. Remove from the heat and add the chocolate and cannabutter. Leave until melted, stirring several times until smooth.

TURN into a bowl and add the liqueur. Chill for several hours or overnight until firm.

SPRINKLE plenty of unsweetened cocoa on a large plate. Take a teaspoonful of the chocolate mixture, roll it lightly in the palm of your hand, and coat the ball in the cocoa. Alternatively, sprinkle spoonfuls of chocolate with the cocoa powder.

ARRANGE the truffles in individual paper cups or pile them on a serving dish. Store in a very cool place or in the refrigerator for up to 2 days.

MARSHMALLOW
CANNABIS SQUARES

PREPARATION TIME: 10 minutes, plus setting
COOKING TIME: 5 minutes

28 white marshmallows, halved
3 tablespoons cannabutter, diced (see page 9)
3½ cups crispy rice cereal
Pink sugar sprinkles, to decorate

*Makes
14 squares
(4 per dose)*

GREASE an 8 x 8 x 2-inch baking pan and line with nonstick parchment paper.

RESERVE 8 of the marshmallows. Put 2 tablespoons of the cannabutter and the remaining marshmallows into a saucepan and heat very gently until melted. Remove from the heat and stir in the rice cereal until evenly coated.

SPOON the mixture into the baking pan and pack down firmly with the back of a spoon.

PUT the remaining cannabutter and reserved marshmallows in a small saucepan and heat gently until melted. Drizzle into the pan in lines, then sprinkle the sugar sprinkles over the top. Let cool for 2 hours, or until firm.

TURN out of the pan onto a board, peel off the lining paper and cut into small squares.

INDEX